Sunflowers

Victoria Blakemore

For Mom, with love and happy memories made in our

sunflower kitchen

Copyright info/picture credits

Table of Contents

What Are Sunflowers?

Sunflowers are tall plants. They can be many different shades of yellow, red, orange, and brown. Some sunflowers are more than one color.

There are over sixty different kinds of sunflowers. They differ in size, color, and where they can be grown.

Sunflowers got their name from

the fact that they turn towards

the sun.

History

Sunflowers originally came from the Americas. They were grown by Native Americans around the area that is now Arizona and New Mexico.

The seeds were ground into flour for bread or mixed with beans and squash. Seeds were also used to dye cloth.

Sunflowers were brought to Europe by Spanish explorers around the year 1500.

Sunflowers became very popular in Russia. Many sunflowers were grown just to make oil from the seeds.

In the late 1800's, sunflower seeds were brought back to America by Russian **immigrants**. Americans grew sunflowers and used the seeds to feed **poultry** on farms.

Scientists experimented with sunflowers. They created many different **hybrid** plants.

Life Cycle

First, a seed is planted in soil.

With enough water and

nutrients, it grows into a sprout.

The sprout grows a hard stem

that has leaves and a bud.

The bud develops into the

head. It is made up of the

flowers and seeds.

Sunflowers are some of the fastest growing plants. Some kinds take as little as eighty days to be fully grown.

Seeds

Sunflower seeds have a hard outer layer. This is called the hull. It protects the kernel, which is the part that people eat.

Sunflower seeds are planted in the soil. The plant grows from the seed.

A single sunflower can have

thousands of seeds.

Roots

The roots grow from the seed.

They grow into the soil and help

to **anchor** the plant. They keep it

in place as it grows.

The roots are also responsible for

taking in **nutrients** from the soil.

These **nutrients** help the

sunflower to grow and stay

healthy.

As the roots grow down into the soil, the stem and leave grow up above the soil.

Stems

The stem grows upwards from the seed. The stems are long, thick, and hollow. They grow towards the sun, so they may lean in one direction.

The stem helps to transport water and nutrients from the roots to the other parts of the plant.

Some sunflowers can grow to be

over ten feet tall. Their strong,

thick stems help to support them.

Leaves

Sunflower leaves grow from the stem. They are very large and can feel soft and fuzzy like velvet.

Sunflower leaves have an important job. They make energy from sunlight in a process called **photosynthesis**.

Sunflower leaves need to
be large to soak up a lot of
sunlight.

Flowers

The part that people think of as the flower is actually called the head. The head is made up of many tiny flowers.

Inside the center of the head are the seeds. They are ready to be harvested when the head has turned brown.

The outer yellow petals are called

ray flowers. The inner parts of the

head are the disc flowers.

Pollination

Some sunflowers are able to **pollinate** themselves. They can transfer pollen from one disc flower to another.

The outer ray flowers of a sunflower are brightly colored. This helps to **attract** pollinators. The wind, animals, and people can also pollinate sunflowers.

Pollinators such as bees collect pollen from sunflowers. When they fly to different flowers, they spread the pollen.

Where Are Sunflowers Grown?

Ukraine and Russia grow more sunflowers than any other countries.

In the United States, South Dakota, North Dakota, Kansas, and Colorado grow the most sunflowers. Over 2 billion pounds of sunflowers are grown in the U.S. each year.

Sunflowers usually bloom in the summer.

Uses

There are two kinds of sunflower seeds. Both kinds have many uses. The black seeds are used to make sunflower oil for cooking or used as bird feed.

They are eaten by many kinds of birds. People like to use them in bird feeders and sprinkle them in their yard to attract birds.

The striped seeds are used more for cooking. They can be roasted and eaten, or used in recipes for things like sunflower seed butter, bread, and salads.

Nutrition

Sunflower seeds can be used to make foods such as sunflower oil and sunflower seed butter. They can also be roasted and eaten.

The seeds contain **nutrients** such as vitamin E, vitamin B, and calcium. They also contain **lecithin**, which is a fat that the cells in our body need.

Sunflower oil is healthiest when it is **unrefined**. It has higher levels of vitamin E and **lecithin** than **refined** sunflower oil.

Health Benefits

The **nutrients** in sunflower seeds have many health benefits. They can help to keep your skin, blood, and heart healthy.

Vitamin E is important for a healthy immune system. It can keep you from getting sick. It is also important for healthy eyes.

The vitamin E in sunflower seeds can also help to keep your heart healthy.

Recipes

Roasted Sunflower Seeds

Ingredients:

Sunflower seeds   1/4 cup salt

8 cups water

Directions:

1. Mix water and salt. Soak unshelled seeds in salted water overnight.

2. Pat seeds dry.

3. Preheat oven to 300 degrees Fahrenheit. Roast seeds on a baking pan for 30 to 40 minutes, or until golden brown.

Make sure to take the outer shell off of the seeds before eating them.

Sunflower Seed Butter

Ingredients:

6 cups hulled sunflower seeds

1/2 tsp salt

1 tsp vanilla extract (optional)

Directions:

1. Preheat oven to 350 degrees Fahrenheit. Toast seeds on a baking sheet for 20-25 minutes, until golden brown. Allow seeds to cool.

2. Process seeds in a food processor until seeds are creamy.

3. Add the salt and vanilla and process for another minute.

Sunflower seed butter should be stored in an air-tight jar to stay fresh.

Glossary

Anchor: to keep stable or in place

Attract: to cause to come near

Hybrid: the offspring of two plants or animals that are different species

Immigrants: people who leave their country to live in another country

Lecithin: a fatty substance that is found in plants and animals

Nutrient: something that helps people, plants, or animals to grow

Photosynthesis: the process a plant uses to make sunlight into energy

Pollinated: when pollen has been transferred to a flower, allowing it to make seeds

Poultry: chicken, turkeys, and other birds that are raised for meat and eggs

Refined: when something has been processed to make it pure

Unrefined: when something has not been processed to remove impurities

About the Author

Victoria Blakemore is a first grade

teacher in Southwest Florida with a

passion for reading.

You can visit her at

www.elementaryexplorers.com

Also in This Series

Gray Wolves	Sloths	Flamingos	Camels	Koalas	Honey Bees	Pandas
Pangolins	White-Tailed Deer	Orcas	Giraffes	Corn	Meerkats	Echidnas
Walruses	Raccoons	Bald Eagles	Apples	Arctic Foxes	Red Pandas	Cassowaries
Tigers	Ladybugs	Moose	Beluga Whales	Leopards	Elephants	Jellyfish
Binturongs	Lions	Dolphins	Reindeer	Hammerhead Sharks	Hippos	Pumpkins
Peafowl	Chameleons	Florida Panthers	Aye-Ayes	Black Bears	Cheetahs	Manatees
Gingerbread	Polar Bears	Hot Chocolate	Orangutans	Coyotes	Marshmallows	Strawberries

All titles by Victoria Blakemore

Also in This Series

Aardvarks	Mako Sharks	Alligators	Frogs	Hedgehogs	Brown Bears	Bongos
Sea Turtles	Quokkas	Muskrats	Zebras	Red Foxes	Ring-Tailed Lemurs	Platypuses
Anteaters	Kangaroos	Rhinos	Jaguars	Wombats	Capybaras	Gorillas
Cats	Skunks	Butterflies	Dingoes	Snow Leopards	African Wild Dogs	Penguins
Whale Sharks	Wolverines	Warthogs	Caracals	Badgers	Seals	Hummingbirds
Pikas	Humpback Whales	Pumas	Lemonade	Llamas	Tulips	Ostriches
Sunflowers	Fennec Foxes					

Victoria Blakemore

www.ingramcontent.com/pod-product-compliance
Lightning Source LLC
Chambersburg PA
CBHW051254020426
42333CB00025B/3202